YOU CAN MAKE IT...
AS A DJ!

First published in 2003 by Miles Kelly Publishing,
Bardfield Centre, Great Bardfield, Essex CM7 4SL

Printed in Italy

ISBN 1-84236-097-3

2 4 6 8 10 9 7 5 3 1

Editorial Director: Anne Marshall
Project Manager: Lisa Clayden
Production Manager: Estela Godoy
Artwork Commissioning: Bethany Walker
Cover Illustration: Maltings Partnership
Illustration: Mark Davis
Layout Design: Mackerel

www.mileskelly.net
info@mileskelly.net

YOU CAN MAKE IT...
AS A DJ!

by Steve & Alan Parker

Illustrations by Mark Davis

CONTENTS

Dedication

To Jane and Anh

About the authors

The authors, Steve and Alan Parker, have always been torn between animals and music. And in music, Steve has always wavered between playing live and playing music from discs. His real job is writing nature and science books for the family readership. But, of a night, he dons his clubbin' cap and spins some wicked grooves. Actually, he wishes he could, but he has recognized his limits and remains a mainstream rock fan and MC at local pub and town-hall gigs. Alan has cast his net wider, in vinyl techniques, musical styles and geography. He's gigged at drum 'n' bass nights in Central London, including the Hanover Grand and the CC Club, and out west in Harrow.

Introduction

So, why would anyone want to be a DJ?

That's a very tricky question. Obviously, it's not for the adulation – the buzz from 10,000 people at a giant rave, who have all come to see you, shout your name and cheer your every move on the decks.

Neither is it for the general fame of being a DJ-ing celebrity. Who would want the best table in every restaurant, automatic membership of exclusive clubs, endless free gifts and holidays?

It's certainly not for the power. A top DJ can alter the mood on the dance floor and make thousands of people happy, sad, or reflective and, finally, frenzied with excitement.

Surely it would not be for the respect, and the admiration of millions of music-lovers, dancers and clubbers, who hang on your every word and opinion? Or for a place in music history, which YOU earn when YOU create YOUR new style of music or dance floor fashion?

For the money? The successful DJ never worries about prices when shopping, or pensions for retirement. Recording royalties, sponsorships and product endorsements provide for life.

Possibly the attraction might be the gateway that DJ-ing provides into mainstream radio, TV and entertainment? As you climb the ladder of celebrity you could become a compere or chat-show host or announcer. Perhaps you might appear as a guest performer, or play a real instrument in a live band. Even the movies and Hollywood might beckon, with Grammys, Emmys, Brits and hundreds of other awards.

Who could possibly want all of that? Not you, for sure.

Why DJ-ing is great

Proper DJ-ing has many serious and worthwhile attractions. For example, you always seem to spend much more of your hard-earned cash on the latest records than you ever earn from gigs.

You fret about equipment and transport, if the van will break down on the way to a venue or the amplifiers will blow up as the event climaxes. You battle through an icy winter's night to a birthday party booking in a cold hall, then no one turns up because they don't like the birthday boy/girl.

You are assured by the promoter that the audience will be teens–twenties, and they turn out to average 73 years of age. You get harassed by drunks, or stuck in the middle of an argument between those who want line-dancing and those who don't.

Finally you struggle home from the gig as the sun comes up, dog-tired, dissatisfied and unfulfilled, and you wonder – yet again – why the heck you bother.

Who could resist such a glamorous and exciting career as a DJ?

A DJ's story

This book is based on the story of Richard Smith (a.k.a. DJ Beanz). He paid his dues as a DJ in dreary local halls. After a long, hard road, he made it big in the city clubs and became a national hero for millions of dancers, clubbers and party-goers.

(Editor's note: He, Richard Smith, could easily be a she, Rikki Smith. The modern music and entertainment business prides itself on being open to both sexes of every persuasion.)

Music styles

Major dance music styles are explained later in the book. Classic tracks and artists are listed for each style. Like any sorts of lists, these are certain to provoke huge disagreement. But that's part of DJ-ing fun.

Starting Out

DJ - disc jockey. A person who jockeys discs, rides the decks, chooses which pieces of music to play to an audience and when. The person who's in charge of the music when people want to dance.

Getting into the world of the DJ can be very hard. Perhaps you know someone who is influential and able to fast-track you to DJ superstardom. Beanz didn't. But he did have the essential key for success in any career – a burning desire to make it big.

DJ dreams

Beanz was an average teenager from an average town. He had been growing keener on music, and even keener on DJ-ing, for several years. Like many young would-be DJs, he spent his money not on computer games or the latest trainers but on records and equipment. The first part of Beanz' dream was to obtain the classic DJ 'starter kit' of a pair of decks (twin vinyl turntables or CD players) and mixer (mixing desk). These can all be bought second-hand for less than the price of just one trainer of a certain brand.

Beanz dreamed of a massive sound system, with a mixing desk like the flight deck of a jumbo jet and speakers as big as houses. To begin, however, his parents' household hi-fi system would do.

Beanz also began to delve into DJ magazines and websites. There are hundreds of these, and they have more information than you could ever imagine about equipment, techniques, venues, big stars, tricks of the trade, latest sounds and more.

DJ-ing in the bedroom

Beanz started off like many real DJs. He sat in his bedroom, playing with his decks and mixer, hour after hour. He began to learn the basics of mixing and scratching (see page 50), trying to blend or merge records together. This involves listening to the details of the rhythm and tempo (speed) of the music, how the different instruments are used, the way melodies work, how songs are structured with verses, choruses, instrumental solos, mood breaks and other features.

Records

Beanz also listened to the charts, hanging around demonstration headphones in big record stores. But he shunned the popular music top ten, and concentrated on the more specialized dance music charts. Most larger towns and cities have specialist dance music record stores. Their staff try to part you from your money, of course. But many are also genuine dance music enthusiasts and willing to share their knowledge. If they make a convert to the dance and club scene, they have a new customer. Also some of them DJ at local clubs. This is exactly what Beanz wanted – contacts in the business.

Equipment

Most larger towns and cities also have sound-system and disco–equipment centres. They sell or hire PA (public address) and sound–reinforcement systems, mixers, decks, lights, smoke machines, microphones and all manner of accessories. The staff are sometimes too liberal with techno-terms such as watts, ohms, XLR plugs and DMX links. But again, some of them may DJ at local clubs, and can become valuable contacts.

In the record store or equipment centre, there's often a noticeboard with adverts for second-hand records, equipment, gigs, agents, promoters and even DJs.

Beanz soaked it all up. But he decided to keep his DJ-ing secret from his friends at school and around the neighbourhood. Then at his first gig, he would amaze them with his skills and level of expertise. They'd rush to book him for their parties and events. However, as we shall see, this secrecy was a less-than-wise move.

First attempt

Gradually Beanz improved his skills on his DJ starter kit of twin decks and mixer. He negotiated with his parents to use the household hi-fi system. He felt ready to cut his teeth on a first event. The more informal, the better – people would not expect too much.

A girl that Beanz quite liked was planning her birthday party. Beanz let it slip that he had some records and sound gear, and that if he was persuaded, he might show up. The girl and her gang were slightly doubtful about semi-nerd Beanz, who had a reputation for hiding away in his bedroom every evening. But they agreed to Beanz' suggestion. If it went well, then great. If Beanz was cack, they could laugh instead.

Not a success

Beanz planned out his music set with military precision. He would feature the latest underground sounds and a couple of show-off tricky turntable manoeuvres. But, as you've guessed, the party was not a success.

Lots of people were invited, but only a few came. The birthday girl was not quite as popular as she imagined. Worse still was Beanz' underground music. It would have gone down a storm in a big city dance venue. But for his audience of average school kids in an average town, it was too obscure, unfamiliar and inaccessible. The party-goers just wanted the latest popular chart hits and golden oldies. They asked for tunes that Beanz

15

didn't have. Also, Beanz had practised his microphone voice in the privacy of his bedroom. But in front of an audience, he was so nervous that he stumbled over words and forgot what to play.

This was a severe lesson. Beanz had the knowledge, the latest grooves and the turntable manoeuvres. He understood the music. What he did not understand was his audience – the type of people, the social situation, and what they might want.

DJ Rule Number One: Know Your Audience.

ǫʊĭℤ

SO YOU WANT TO BE A DJ?

*Try this simple quiz to assess your future as
a star DJ. Remember that if you answer all
the questions honestly, you're not really true
DJ material.*

1 **The night is in full swing – and
   someone leans on the house lights
   switch. The resulting brightness ruins
   the mood. Do you:**

   A Take no action, hoping someone will
      turn them off again.

   B Make a quick joke into the
      microphone, tell the person to turn
      the lights off again, then resume your
      set, having pointed out who was
      responsible for the gaff (not you).

   C Have security remove the person and
      ban them for life from the venue.

2 **On the way to your first major gig in a big club, your records are misplaced. (That is, you forget them.) What do you do?**

A Stay at home, hoping no one will notice.

B Ask around every local record shop to see if you can borrow a few tunes.

C Phone up the promoter, agent or venue and explain the situation.

3 **Someone approaches you in the middle of a house-shakin' set and asks for a record you don't have (but perhaps should). What do you say?**

A Apologize and suggest something similar.

B Say you'll play it later, hoping they forget.

C Tell them to leave you alone, you play what you want!

4 **Somebody collapses on the dance floor. A crowd of people gathers. It looks serious. You are in charge and must choose a course of action. Do you:**

A Leap over the decks and attempt to perform mouth-to-mouth resuscitation.

B Stop the music and get on the mike, with the time-honoured 'Is there a doctor in the house?', and ask for expert help or an ambulance.

C Ignore the person and carry on playing.

5 **The record you are playing starts to skip or jump. People look up at you in annoyance. Do you:**

A Immediately fade it out and put something else on, since you always have an emergency track lined up, ready to go.

B Leave it, hoping it will sort itself out.

C Blame it on the decks and storm off in a fit of rage.

6 **It's the end of a good night, everyone has had a wicked time. You approach the promoter for your money, as arranged, but the promoter laughs. You should be grateful that you were allowed to play at all! Time for action, so do you:**

A Immediately suggest a much lower price than was originally offered.

B Thank the promoter with a forced smile for such generosity and leave with gritted teeth.

C Politely insist that you are paid, as you had all agreed.

7 **In the middle of a pumpin' set, there's an urgent call from nature, and the toilets are on the far side of the packed dance floor! Do you:**

A Ask your best mate to look after the set for you until you return.

B Put on a really long track, and ask security to ensure no one goes near the decks.

C Stop the record, tell everyone that it's time for the food/raffle/speeches, and dash off to be as quick as you can in the can.

Answers

1 *A-2, B-3, C-1. There's a balance between staying popular among your audience and keeping the night going, while at the same time appearing in control.*

2 *A-1, B-3, C-2. Enthusiasm to play, whatever happens, is a great asset. But if there's really no way you can do it, then tell people in advance.*

3 *A-3, B-2, C-1. Trying to please everyone all the time is not easy. But an attempt is better than arrogance or making enemies. (See also pages 58–60.)*

4 *A-2, B-3, C-1. Be aware of what's going down on the dance-floor. However, DJs are rarely qualified doctors. Show concern, act quickly, then leave it to the professionals.*

5 *A-3, B-2, C-1. Trusting to luck does not always work, and neither does a fit of rage. The crowd will soon forget if the set storms onwards.*

6 *A-2, B-1, C-3. Successful DJ-ing is a skilled job and the crowd have had several hours of entertainment. That's worth money – and respect.*

7 *A-1, B-3, C-2. Entrusting your reputation to a mate, who might interrupt the flow of the set, is less desirable than a planned withdrawal.*

How did you score?

1-7   *Bar-work or shelf-stacking is always attractive.*

8-14   *Your DJ-ing strategy is taking shape. Stick with it.*

15-21 *Order that Ferrari now!*

Gig Guide

Beanz would soon find out that all gigs are not the same. There are at least a hundred types of event where a DJ encounters the public. They vary in the way that something which is extremely variable varies – like, say, the weather.

Each gig follows a general pattern for its type. Beanz eventually came to write his own gig guide, featuring about a dozen of the main types of event. But each gig is the same in that it's unique. That's the DJ's challenge.

Sports club bash

This type of gig can vary from the under-15s hockey squad to the over-60s beach volleyball team. However, if the venue is the team's regular clubhouse or HQ, many guests will be on home ground. They feel relaxed and among friends, ready to go under the influence of inexpensive drinks. So the dance-floor can fill with surprising speed. However, the audience often peak too soon. Several hours later they are still on the floor, but horizontal. Sadly, a few drinks may be thrown in anger. Sports where this can happen, from most glasses hurled to least, are footy, rugger, cricket, tennis, rowing, judo and boxing.

Kiddies' fun-tabulous playtime event

The DJ must brush up on junior party games such as statues, musical chairs and pass-the-parcel. Adoring parents pretend that they don't mind when their child loses, but secretly they are in fierce competition. So microphone announcements, especially when identifying game winners, need great diplomacy. The afternoon party is a very unnatural time for the DJ to work, or even be awake. Also most of the kiddy guests want cartoon theme tunes, but there's always one little devil who requests Hardcore House, so that he can snigger at the explicit lyrics. Balloons, jellies and ice-cream provide a break, but as the event wanes, some overheated toddler is sick behind the speaker. The kiddy party always ends in tears.

School bop

End-of-term is the usual excuse for a school dance, but it can be post-exams, or a sporting achievement. If the venue is the school hall, which is usually a gymnasium too, then the high ceiling, hard walls, wooden floor and plentiful windows cause nightmare acoustics. They also make it impossible to achieve mood lighting or any kind of atmosphere. Announcements should be v-e-r-y-s-l-o-wa-n-d-c-l-e-a-r or the words echo round and round in the ceiling. The music is usually overshadowed by playground politics, who fancies who, who looks a cheap slut and who's a mummy's boy.

Chair-ee-dee fundraiser

Charity events are often dominated by earnest people who know nothing about music or dancing. They turn up to 'do good'. Having bought an entry ticket, raffle ticket, prize-draw ticket and 'done their bit', they disappear early. There's often loads of announcing for the DJ to do, such as the raffle, the amount of money raised, the 67 people and organizations who donated prizes and so on. A wise DJ avoids such tiring talk, and asks the organizers to find an eminent member of the committee for the task. Then the DJ can concentrate on the music. The saving grace is that, whatever happens, it's all in a good cause.

Teenage party at home

This usually has very subdued lighting, or none at all, while anxious parents fret in the next room. Every third request from the floor is for the slowest, sexiest ballad in the charts, so that the snogging can recommence. A particular challenge is when some smart, budding music buff asks for one of the latest underground Hardcore tracks, to try and catch out the DJ. Even if you have the track, and play it to maintain respect, no one else will know it and the mood could die. Like the kiddies' party, this type of gig always ends in tears, and with someone throwing up – usually cider-and-alcopop shandy and kebab, rather than lemonade and jelly.

Wedding reception

Tricky indeed, due to the huge age-range, and the probability that many guests are relative strangers. Older family members often haven't seen each other for centuries. They want to gossip and catch up. So a bit of ballroom dancing early on, like a waltz, can ease the DJ's plight. Also included here are the latest kiddy chart hits for the young bridesmaids and pageboys. Remember that youngsters and

wrinklies have had a long day, and will soon tire. Liaise with the best man, the venue owner, the bride's father or whoever is in charge, about the schedule, food, speeches and other interruptions. Do the happy couple have a special song for their first outing on the dance floor? Choose some Cheese for their departure, as guests raise their arms and link hands to make the traditional tunnel. The fun can end abruptly at this point – or the gig can really get going.

Birthday or anniversary party

This is usually one of the more audience age-specific gigs. Unless it's a 100th, many of the guests will be within a year or two of the birthday girl or boy – 18, 21, 40 or whatever.

Consult a music-charts-over-the-years book to find danceable pop tunes from significant times in the past: when the birthday girl or boy was born, turned 18, got married, and endured other life events. This gives a

framework around which you can build a session. Also consult the same book for hit tunes from the years when most guests were in their mid-teens. This is usually the 'growing up' era with the fondest musical memories. But, before accepting the gig in the first place, consider if the birthday girl/boy is popular. If you were invited as a guest, would you go to the party? If not – beware.

Wake

This is something of a valuable rarity. The release of emotion at a funeral, and the 'Old-Ronnie-would-have-wanted-a-good-send-off' factor, can turn it into a rip-roarin' night. However, if the festivities continue for too long people have the chance to turn depressed and maudlin, as they fill up with cheap drink and limp cheese. So the DJ quits while the going is good and the mood is still elevated. A swift one-ballad ending and a final good night is one favoured option.

Local fête or outdoor fair

A flexible DJ can be persuaded to act as MC or announcer for the afternoon fête or fair, as well as the evening disco or dance. But this makes a very long day and night. Music with outdoor associations helps to make the scene swing, such as jigs, reels, Big Beat and summery holiday hits. However, several factors on this type of gig are outside the DJ's control, primarily the weather, and noise complaints from Mrs Growler who lives across the road.

Proper dance or disco club
Now we're getting somewhere. Read on.

The Dance Experience

Beanz was shaken by the lack of success at his first gig, but not downhearted. After all, to succeed as a DJ you must have plenty of self-confidence. He decided to visit his local disco-equipment centre to cheer himself up. He wanted to buy a pair of proper headphones. The DJ uses these to listen in 'privately' and hear what's playing, on various inputs at the mixer, without the sounds coming through the main speakers.

DJ's best friend

The store had an interesting-looking pair of second-hand headphones. Beanz tried them and they fitted exceptionally well. The cups seal around the ears, to keep out the blare of the main sound system when required. Many DJs hold one cup of the 'phones to one ear, to cue or line up the next track, while listening with the other 'open' ear, to what's playing through the main sound system.

A voice from nowhere

Beanz idly twiddled the headphone volume control, but his mind was elsewhere. It was a shame about yesterday's gig. What had gone so wrong? Suddenly the headphones gave out a strange cackling sound, and a small, clear robot-like voice spoke: *DJ Rule Number One: Know Your Audience.*

Beanz was so startled that for a second he forgot to look cool. He cast a suspicious eye over the mixer for unusual wires or a radio microphone. All seemed normal. He took off the 'phones, checked them, and cautiously put them on again. The small computer-like voice spoke again: *DJ Rule Number Two: Know Your Music!*

Beanz could not believe his ears. They must be magic

headphones, responding to his thoughts! He went through the question again, slowly and clearly, in his own mind. What had gone wrong with yesterday's gig?

It was the wrong type of music for the event. You played Hardcore House and trippy Garage, best suited to keen clubbers. But your listeners were ordinary young people who just wanted popular chart tunes.

A helping hand

Beanz bought the magic headphones. They had been owned by top DJs in the past, and could pass on invaluable advice. But he had to ask the right questions by thinking slowly and clearly. One of the headphones' pieces of advice was: *Experience a disco club from the dance floor.* This would help him to understand what the crowd wants, at different types of gigs. A very good point, thought Beanz. He'd been alone in his bedroom far too long. He must see an event from the consumer's viewpoint. So the very next evening, Beanz and a friend visited the local dance club. This is what they found.

Off to the club

Most club nights start around 10pm. Generally, if you arrive at 9–9.30pm, you'll be near the front of the queue to beat the rush, get in early and grab that oh-so-precious table with seats. After 11pm, the line of expectant dancers may go around the block. Most clubs also have a shut-off time for last entry. And when the limit on crowd capacity is reached, it's a 'one in, one out' policy.

Some places have a strict dress code, others are more casual and flexible. But if there is a code, stick to it. Trading off trainers against a shirt-with-collar is rarely allowed.

In the queue

Queuers are often annoyed when selected people stroll straight to the front, being welcomed with smiles and open arms. They are on the guest list! Sometimes the famous DJ arrives, accompanied by henchmen carrying record boxes.

These sights made Beanz even more determined to make it big. One day HE would write the guest list.

The queue frustration was eased by chatting to fellow clubbers about the night in store. As Beanz neared the entrance, the muffled bass beat throbbed from within. At the door, the staff gave a quick body-pat search and peered into bags and pockets. Beanz paid up and finally walked down the stairs, to the club itself.

On the floor

The first hit was the NOISE. Beanz could barely hear himself think. The club atmosphere is usually dark and smoky, with flashing lights, and people pushing and shouting. Time for the next decision. Do you join another queue for the bar, or circle the floor to eye up the dancers, or plunge straight into the groove yourself? Or do you stand around, yelling at your mates, 'WHAT DO YOU WANNA DO?'

Most clubs have a schedule or poster showing the time-slots for each DJ. Generally the early sessions are taken up by the lesser names or the club's resident DJ. Later, when the venue has filled, the big stars come out.

At the DJ booth

In most clubs, DJs work in a booth, on a plinth or behind a big desk, elevated from the floor and perhaps screened by glass panels. Beanz joined the people crowded here. These DJ-watchers have differing agendas. Some want to know the records, or watch the DJ's turntable manoeuvres. Some just want to see a famous DJ close up, and maybe comment on the set. A few might be trainspotter-type record fanatics who want to 'tick' the latest tracks on their lists.

In a big club with a star DJ, requests from the public are rare. You cannot get physically close enough to ask, and you cannot shout because the music is too loud. In any case, most clubbers are there to experience and respect the DJ's work and judgement, rather than to hear what others might suggest. Beanz understood this at once. He watched, listened and learned.

Dance floor caricatures

Out on the dance floor, most people just do their own thing. But there are several classic dancing types who crop up at almost every venue.

The master-dancer or break-dancer, especially at Hip Hop clubs, whose bodyflips and headspins are praised by encircling onlookers.

 The sweaty, unshirted raver, with wild eyes and erratic body movements, who crashes painfully into those nearby.

 Head-nodders and foot-tappers, usually standing at the edge of the main floor, looking cool and controlled.

 The lurve gods and goddesses, who dance not so much for their own fun, as to let others gaze admiringly at them.

Towards the let-down

Beanz felt fully at home. The whole dance club experience was fuelling his desire to become a DJ superstar. Soon it would be time for one of his favourites, DJ Hasn't-Turned-Up, to rock the decks. But, calamity – he hasn't turned up! Shocking! Yet actually quite common. Famous DJs often play several sets in one night, in different clubs. They can be delayed by travel problems or breakdowns, just like anyone else.

Beanz was disappointed. However, one of the earlier DJs heroically stepped in, and began to work the crowd. The dancers pushed themselves to new levels of energy as wicked tracks blasted from the speakers and the MC (Master of Ceremonies) rapped up a frenzy. Suddenly the DJ dropped in a classic rave track, and everyone went wild – they felt like one big, happy, noisy family. Beanz was witnessing the rise of a new star DJ. He knew, more than ever, that he would be next.

DJ phrase generator

Use the handy DJ phrase generator (opposite) to say the right thing at all times. Choose one entry from each column, but mix up the rows for thousands of fab combinations to begin your show:

'Yeah, we're gonna be rinsin' out a wagon-load of House-style dangerous cuts.'

No one knows exactly what you mean, but they all get the general idea.

Cut-out-and-keep DJ Phrase chart

INSTANT COOL PHRASES!

Mixin' up	a dose of	phat	clubbin'	rhythms
Layin' down	a wagon-load of	classic	slammin'	cuts
Spinnin'	a bunch of	wicked	dance-floor	vibes
Droppin'	an onslaught of	House-style	funky	beats
Throwin'	a big batch of	bangin'	party	grooves
Blendin'	a raft of	havin'-it	cookin'	tracks
Playin'	a trench of	massive	disco	discs
Rinsin' out	a pl-pl-plethora of	largin'-it	pile-drivin'	numbers
Bustin'	a six-pack of	fun-tabulous	rave-tastic	songs
Grabbin'	a shedful of	burnin'	dangerous	tunes

Big Break

After his first time at a real dance club, Beanz was tired but elated. He visited again and again, to appreciate the varying styles of music on different nights. He wanted to study how the big-name DJs watched the dance floor, soaked up the mood, and used various techniques to motivate the crowd, get them onto the floor, boost them into a frenzy and then let them down slowly. As the magic headphones advised, learn and gain experience whenever you can.

Club mechanics

Beanz also took in the layout and mechanics of the club, and how it was organized. With the help of his headphones, his regular DJ magazines, and visits to numerous websites, he learned about sound systems, and the placing of the speakers and lights. He savoured the chill-out area where tired punters could escape from the frantic pace of the dance floor. He gazed enviously at the VIP area for the DJs, promoters, club owners and special guests. He saw how the star names always appeared cool, calm and collected at all times.

Filling the floor

A classic DJ challenge is to how to get people onto the dance floor. This applies not so much at proper clubs, where guests have paid to rave and are 'up for it'. It's chiefly a problem for the mobile DJ or small club, when the crowd is thin and unfamiliar with the disco scene. Few people want to be first on the dance floor, exposed to the embarrassing eyes of curious onlookers.

● If the audience are all much the same age, play a couple of chart tracks from the years when they would have been in their mid-to late teens. Music from this 'coming of age' time brings back fond memories.

- For a mixed age group, rattle through several popular music styles such as classic 70s Disco, modern Hip Hop, Old Skool 'rave' or Rock 'n' Roll. Watch for  encouraging signs such as tapping feet and mouthing words, and build on these styles.

- Play an ultra-famous track from the 'Cheese selection' (see page 75). Most people will groan, flick their eyes heavenwards – but then shuffle onto the floor.

- On the microphone, direct a few comments at individuals or groups. A couple of 'good sports' in the audience usually withstand teasing: 'Sheila and Paul, this one's been requested specially for you, so let's see those feet twinkle.' Or 'We wanna see all the grannies up and dancing – with their grandsons!'

- At a birthday, wedding or similar, use one of the chief guests as a name-who-must-beobeyed. 'This is specially for the best man, Jim. He says you've all gotta get up and dance!'

- Just occasionally, a hastily organized dancing competition will break the ice, with something as simple as a bottle for the prize.

Emptying the floor

Just as challenging as the floor-fill, is the floor-empty at the end of the night. Cries of 'More, more!' are very gratifying for the DJ, but not when the club owner is staring hard and the staff, brooms poised, want to go home.

- Plan ahead. Try to peak the action about 15 minutes before switch-off. Then you have time to slow the pace gradually with a couple of ballads.

- Tell them the next track is definitely final, when you've really allowed yet another few minutes for the extra 'last blast'.

- Turn on the house lights – a time-honoured signal that the end is nigh.

- For the persistent 'Why can't you play just one more?', have a firm statement based on licensing laws, noise complaints, bylaws

of the venue or similar semi-official reasons.
In other words – blame it on someone else.

- Get someone else, like the club owner,
  promoter or venue hirer, to tell everyone –
  that's your lot!

The big chance

Beanz became a regular at the local dance
club. With his increasing knowledge, turntable
skills and magic headphones, he now felt
ready to try his hands on the decks. But how?

- Personal route – befriend a couple of local
  DJs and promoters. A casual word here and
  there would show you are interested and in
  the know. But never appear too keen or let
  your 'mask of cool' slip.

- Cold call – send in or drop off a CD (or
  tape) which you've made, at the club. This
  demonstrates your music selection and
  mixing skills.

- 'Open decks' – put your name down for one of the nights when first-timers or newcomers are allowed a short session.

- Radio – check out the local radio stations and see if you can get a starter session which gives the station free air time.

Beanz followed a vital rule of DJ-ing: Take no chances. He did all of the above. And one night, he found himself in the hallowed position on the podium, vinyl at his fingertips, trusty magic headphones on, crowd expectant and ready to go. This was his big break.

CHOOSE YOUR FORMAT

- CDs (compact discs) are small, light, easy to carry, fairly reliable and excellent quality, with a vast choice of recordings. However, they are susceptible to vibration, dust, damage and unpredictable skips. Some argue that CD sound is too 'cold' and 'precise', and there's little physical control over the discs. However, specialist CD decks allow you to alter pitch, jog, do instant starts and even scratch.

- Vinyl (black plastic record) is still the chosen format for professional club DJs. It allows huge physical control of the sound (see Turntablism, page 50). Also, vinyl is often the only format for really underground or hardcore tracks, whose makers shun putting their work on 'woossy' CDs.

● Computer DJ-ing (PC-DJ) allows a vast amount of music to be stored on hard disc. Set-up time at a gig is short, with fewer plugs. Some DJ programs attempt to simulate real turntables, with control of speed, pitch and other features. However, is sitting in front of a computer as much fun as standing by the decks, pumping your fist with the crowd?

● MiniDiscs (like CDs but smaller) have never really replaced CDs, but they are a useful home recording medium for making your own tracks.

DISCO-'TECH' – WATTS, SUBS AND BELS

Some DJs get involved in the technical side of the business. Others don't. They leave it to their roadies or 'equipment guys'.

WATT Power from the main amplifiers, which drive the main speakers. The number of watts is a guide to loudness and sound quality. The more watts, the better for both. 1,000 watts is tolerable at a small-hall venue, say 50–100 people. 10,000 watts and up is club status, with midriff-penetrating bass. So watts are great. But they cost money and they need bigger, heavier speakers. For the mobile DJ, this can be a drag.

SUB There are several types of speakers – horns and tweeters (small) for high-pitched sounds, woofers and subwoofers or bass bins (very big) for low, deep sounds. The subwoofer's sounds are so low, ears hardly register them. But they turn your intestines to jelly.

DECIBEL A unit of sound intensity (dB) or loudness. Above 85–90 dB is pretty noisy, above 100 dB extremely so. Many venues have local regulations to limit sound systems output and the public's exposure, since hearing damage is always a risk.

Tricks of the Trade

Beanz' first session at the Club MissTake was a
moderate success. Over the previous weeks his
friends had noticed changes. Beanz had
emerged from his bedroom and found a
proper social life. So they turned up in support
and were mildly amazed. Was this the shy
stutterer who, just a few months ago, had
baffled them at the neighbourhood birthday
bash? Beanz' mates decided to become his
gang or posse. If he did become a DJ
superstar, some of the fame and glamour
might reflect onto them.

A new identity

The magic headphones continued to give
Beanz sensible advice. One piece was: *Get a*

name. You may recall that Beanz' real name was Richard Smith. So far, he had not changed it. Now, as the 'phones said, it needed some thought.

A DJ's name can be – anything. It might have links with music, dance, discos and clubs, or it might not. It could be preceded by a title such as DJ or MC, or not. It might have strange spelling as an added attraction, and be a touch self-mocking, like DJ Phat-Soh, or not.

Choosing a name

The DJ's name should conjure up feelings of mystery, toughness, coolness, darkness, being on the edge and 'out there'. It must NOT sound soft, fluffy, yielding, flexible or lightweight. For example, DJ Cotton Wool would be less groovy than DJ Steel Wire.

Some DJs simply use their own real name. Beanz considered this, but DJ Richard was not quite right. He also thought about using his surname, but DJ Smith did not seem to fit the criteria either.

Then one day, as he was eating beans on toast, an idea came. Beans! He was, after all, full of beans. And that was how much he earned, too. It was short, snappy, easily spelled and difficult to mishear. Maybe he might tweak the spelling. DJ Beanz it was.

Turntablism

Turntablism encompasses scratching and mixing skills. It requires much practice and some top DJs spend several hours daily on the art of using the record decks and mixer like an instrument. The best turntablists compete every year at international DJ championships, and there are hundreds of local events. Judges award points in several areas such as beat-juggling and specialist scratches (see below), overall creativity, presentation and so on.

There are even team events, each member has a deck and mixer and 'plays' an instrument or part, just like a band with musical instruments. Each DJ's scratching technique is unique, and physical mastery of the decks is the holy grail of many would-be DJs.

Scratch-mixing

In scratching, which originated in the 1970s, the rotation of a vinyl disc is manipulated with the hands and fingers. The disc can be speeded, slowed, stopped, reversed, etc. with the stylus (needle) in the groove. With a suitable original recording, this produces some very strange sound-effects. It's also used to coordinate the rhythm between two recordings on different decks, so that one can be merged seamlessly into the other.

'Scratching' denotes the classic 'eek-kee-eek-kee' noise produced when the portion of the groove containing a sharp sound, like a drum snap, is moved to and fro past the stylus.

However, most scratching involves one hand on the disc and one on the mixing desk, usually moving the crossfader (see page 91).

Scratching appals hi-fi buffs. It means actually touching the sacred surface of a vinyl disc, and smearing it with sweat and skin flakes. It also moves the groove in reverse direction past the stylus – sacrilege!

Deck moves

 Baby scratch The simplest scratch is to move the disc back and forth with your hand, without changing the mixer volume or crossfader. This produces the classic scratchy sound, like a fingernail rubbed to and fro along the teeth of a comb. But there are countless patterns and variations. In 'tears' the record is moved forward then stopped, then moved forwards again.

 Stabs or chops A portion or sample of the recording is repeatedly played one way, flicking the crossfader over to the other side to get rid of the sound as the sample goes backwards in between. For example 'yeeaah' would sound like 'ye-ye-ye-ye'. This is a common and relatively easy move, as both your hands work naturally in coordination.

 Chirps The record is moved forwards with the crossfader open, so you can hear the sound, then the crossfader is closed (moved across) to silence the part where you quickly stop the disc and start to move it backwards. Then open the fader again so that the same sound repeats but with the record now going backwards. In this way you catch a piece of sound both forwards and backwards, but without the split-second slow-down, stop and speed-up in reverse.

Crabbing The crab involves flicking the crossfader sideways with each finger in turn, in fast succession. Start with your little finger and end with your index finger, so your fingers look like a crab walking. It's similar to drumming fingers on a table. The fader springs back after each flick and the effect is to turn the volume up and down extremely fast, once with each flick, to produce a quick succession of short sounds, 'a-a-a-a-a-a-ahhhhhh'.

 Orbit The same number of flicks or clicks on the crossfader are done forwards and then backwards. So a two-click orbit could sound like 'ah-ah' (forwards) and then straight away 'ha-ha' (backwards).

 Flare This tricky move means going against your natural hand movements. You move the record forwards, swish or click the fader off then on again, then move the record back and do the same. The change in direction of the record, which you don't normally hear in a stab, is now audible, 'EhWeh-WehEh'. In effect, you can scratch twice as fast, since you are not creating the sounds with the crossfader alone. You hear the sounds on both sides of the fader click.

Gigs Galore

DJ Beanz was 'on the up' at last. His sessions at the Club MissTake drew more admirers. His track selection and turntable action improved, and his fame spread. The magic headphones continued to give invaluable help, especially in gauging the type of music going down well.

But no sooner had Beanz put one foot on the ladder than the club suffered a fire and had to close for renovation. This was disaster. How could Beanz keep up the momentum? To continue the path to stardom, he needed another dance club – or to go on the road.

MC Toast, one of the DJs from a local mobile disco, had seen Beanz and liked his style. Toast was an expert rapper and MC. 'Toasting' is the name of a type of rapping, using rapid syllables, sounds and clicks that fit into the music. Toast reckoned that Beanz with his mixing and turntable skills would complete a groove duo. Was it fate that MC Toast linked up with DJ Beanz, to form Beanz'n'Toast?

Going mobile

The mobile disco is a different animal from the dance club. Gone are the familiar faces, the comfy surroundings, and carrying just a record box. Each gig is in different surroundings and acoustics. There's plenty of physical work both before and after the event, lugging speakers and amplifiers and lights and stands. Setting up the gear and breaking it down (taking it apart) can take longer than the event in between. The audience is not always enthusiastic. Some are there on sufferance, forced to attend by well-meaning friends or relatives.

Excuses

Beanz found the mobile disco hard at first. But it was good training in assessing crowds and thinking on his feet. In particular, the mobile DJ needs excuses. This is because the audience contains a vast array of people, of different ages and tastes – but the disco can only carry limited recordings.

Excuses are needed mainly when punters request tracks that the DJ doesn't have. But an impossible request is not the end of the world. It's time for quick thinking. The able DJ quickly sum up the situation: the age and condition of the requester, the stage of the evening, the type of audience and which styles of music have gone well so far.

Rebuffs

These are delivered in a confident, almost nonchalant way, with no further discussion expected. The DJ says the words and goes straight back to choosing discs or adjusting mixer controls:

'That track is with our other disco, which is busy elsewhere.'

'Yes, it's really popular, we'll play it near the

end.' (You hope the requester forgets, gets drunk or goes home.)

'The request list is already very long but we'll do our best.'

'It will fit the mood in about 20 minutes.'

'We'll try to play it in the next segment.'

Sometimes the request is more forceful, not to say aggressive. Use caution here, with nods and smiles, and promises that you'll do your best:

'We'll certainly try to squeeze it in. But if we haven't got that, what would be your second choice?'

Put-downs

Another batch of excuses stamps the DJ's authority on the proceedings. But they should be used with caution against musclebound hunks with many tattoos who request Motorhead or Wu-Tang Clan.

'We've already played that one.' (To be used

if the requester is drunk enough to believe it –
or if you actually have already played it.)

'We'll put that on while the food's being
served.'

'Maybe you could go home and get it.'

'We only play quality tunes.'

'We don't carry that one any more – no one's
asked for it for ages.'

Mime

Another option for excuses
involves simple mime.
First, pretend that the
music is too loud, or
hurriedly put on your
headphones. Then in
reply to a shouted
demand, you nod and
smile, or grimace and break
out into a grin, or give the thumbs-up sign to
indicate all's well.

Use audience reaction in your favour. If the
dance floor is full, indicate the fact with a
wave of your hand. Imply that it's best not to
disturb the mood with an obscure request,
since everyone is having such a great time.

The big league

Jobbing DJs who run mobile set-ups or small clubs cope regularly with awkward enquiries. When you don't have to battle with requesters any more – you're big league. Most famous big-name DJs play their own style, and are known for playing that style. People come for precisely that reason.

A toast to success

As Beanz'n'Toast grew in fame, this is exactly what they found. A rising star generates buzz, which creates more publicity, and so on, in a self-stoking cycle. Demand soared for the Beanz'n'Toast mobile. When the Club

MissTake reopened, they were asked to the grand first night. Gradually they worked their way up the bill to the coveted late-night Saturday (i.e. Sunday morning) slot. Beanz and his magic headphones seemed unstoppable. He was then asked to guest at a major club in the big city. He was up, up and away.

The sound system set-up

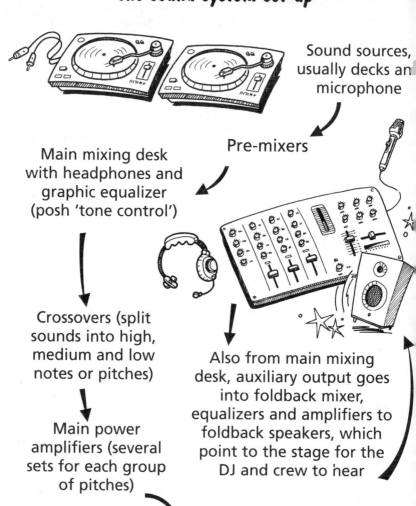

Sound sources, usually decks and microphone

Pre-mixers

Main mixing desk with headphones and graphic equalizer (posh 'tone control')

Crossovers (split sounds into high, medium and low notes or pitches)

Main power amplifiers (several sets for each group of pitches)

Also from main mixing desk, auxiliary output goes into foldback mixer, equalizers and amplifiers to foldback speakers, which point to the stage for the DJ and crew to hear

Main banks of loudspeakers for dance floor (ditto)

The sounds of silence

What should you do if the sound system suddenly goes pop? It happens to every DJ at some time. Beanz' magic headphones had plenty of advice on this topic.

 Wiggle each plug in each socket in turn, according to a pre-determined plan along the equipment chain. Clicks and cut-outs suggest a faulty lead.

 Bypass a faulty amplifier and redirect the signals to another amp.

 An oddly flickering light can be bashed with the butt end of a screwdriver, which usually works.

 Get the equipment engineer to mend it.

 As an alternative to all of the above, simply check the fuse in the plug at the mains socket. It's nearly always that fuse.

Big in the Biz

As Beanz hit the big time, he began to receive the attentions of the music business. This is a risky time, as the biz takes over from the sounds. Did he need an agent? Also a manager, a promoter, a publicist and an image consultant? They would only take 20 per cent each.

White labels

Beanz began to receive discs from record labels, producers, mixers and artists. These were 'promos' or anonymous-looking 'white labels' – new tracks not yet released to the public. DJs listen to them and play the more interesting ones in their sets. This gets the crowd interested in material they have not yet heard, and shows them that the DJ is truly at the cutting edge of musical fashion.

Creating new vibes

Beanz also worked on impressing the crowd with his mixing and scratching. He wanted to create new sequences that could excite the people more than an individual track. This ability does not come out of thin air. It needs hours of thinking, listening and practising. Gradually you bring rhythms in and out, up and down, round and round, always maintaining interest and intrigue, with quiet moments that build to a peak and then resolve with satisfaction.

What the crowd expect

As the magic headphones kept reminding Beanz, it's vital to know different clubs and venues, and how knowledgeable their crowds are. A few simple scratching moves in the appropriate musical style – Drum 'n' bass, Hip

Hop, Big Beat – can impress the not-too-experienced. More complex manoeuvres and mixes in this situation would lose the listeners. The expert stuff is fine for true enthusiasts, who expect and appreciate bold new moves.

Good behaviour

So much to remember! Another important feature is behaviour behind the decks. Many top DJs jump around and look at the crowd to connect with their public. They smile with enthusiasm and their facial expressions follow the changing moods of the mix. They inspire. The DJ's energy, concentration, pleasure and fun all convey enthusiasm and effort. This is what the public love.

The afterlife

Also ... but there we must leave the tale of DJ

Beanz, as he disappears into the stratosphere. What happened to him? Perhaps he ruined himself with excessive behaviour. Maybe he gradually grew tired of the money and adulation. Possibly he didn't move with the times and faded from the public eye.

On radio or TV

One option for the tiring DJ is radio or television. In fact, many active club DJs also have radio or even TV shows. For some, this combination works fine. But the live club and the broadcast media differ more than you might imagine. The live club involves sweaty dancers packed together, with noise and light, in a physically demanding audio-visual frenzy providing instant

feedback as vibes change through the evening. The broadcast media does not.

Big television and radio networks snap up new DJ talents with wide appeal. There are also hundreds of pirate and semi-pirate radio stations, sometimes several in one city. These can be both start- and end-points. Every week, DJ hopefuls take to the airwaves to play their music and expose their skills. The Internet has also got in on the act. It's possible for small stations to broadcast all over the world via a website.

In the studio

Some DJs move into the recording studio, as an engineer, producer, artist, or all three. DJs who have been recording and producing their own sounds, samples and mixes, and who have built up a reputation, may take this route.

A fresh musical direction may be triggered by age, new trends or simply a desire for change. It's perfectly possible to become bored with playing pumping techno every week, and to utilize your sonic abilities by writing guitar-laden ballads instead.

Change of career

With dosh in the bank after years of tireless service to the music industry, the adventurous DJ may decide to have a more drastic change of career. How about owning a club or pub, a football team or a chain of fashionable clothing outlets?

Staying big in the biz

Of course, some superstar DJs end up doing very little, because they don't have to. Here is one recipe for a long and happy afterlife:

 Recording royalties, which alone amount to a new luxury yacht every second year.

 Marriage to a fellow star from an allied industry, like a girl/boy band, record producer or tag-wrestling team.

 The inevitable autobiography, exposing rival DJs as hideously awful, untalented liars and creeps.

 A weekly spot on the radio, and regular guest slots on TV chat shows with fellow DJs who have become comperes.

 On tour at theatres and clubs, treating audiences to an exclusive question-and-answer session or after-dinner speech.

Such an arduous schedule can be interrupted by regular visits back to your enormous country mansion. You swim in your luxury pool, entertain hand-picked guests, and tinker in your own recording studio with your new 'experimental' stuff – that is, music which other people will never hear.

If all else fails, there's always the option of the come-back gig …

At the peak of his powers, Beanz decided that he no longer needed his magic headphones. From the beginning, he'd had the burning desire, the thoughts and the abilities to become a great DJ. True, the 'phones had advised him well along the way.

But now they were no longer needed. So Beanz asked a friend to part-exchange them, at a disco equipment store in an average small town. Your town? There the headphones wait, for their chance to guide the next keen young Dj to mega-stardom.

Major Dance Music

ACID HOUSE

As classic Disco faded, especially in the USA, the young wanted something new. In 1985 producers Frankie

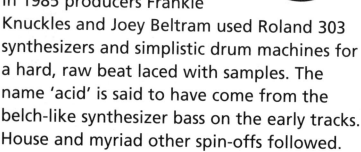

Knuckles and Joey Beltram used Roland 303 synthesizers and simplistic drum machines for a hard, raw beat laced with samples. The name 'acid' is said to have come from the belch-like synthesizer bass on the early tracks. House and myriad other spin-offs followed.

Classic tracks
A Guy Called Gerald – 'Voodoo Ray'
Joey Beltram – 'Energy Flash'
Jungle Brothers – 'I'll House You'
Phuture Acid – 'Trax'
Slam – 'Positive Education'

AMBIENT

Coined by Brian Eno, progressive guitarist and

electronic music wizard (originally in 1970s chart band Roxy Music), the term 'Ambient' describes music to create atmosphere or 'vibes' – ambience. Some is non-rhythmic, unearthly yet restful, with swooping, whooshing synthesized sounds. But Ambient has gone dance too, with a heavier beat underlying the weird soundscapes.

Classic tracks
Air – 'All I Need'
Aphex Twin – 'Selected Ambient Works, vol. 2'
Robert Miles – 'Children'
The Orb – 'Orblivion'

BIG BEAT

Evolving since about 1994, Big Beat has a mixed origin in Hip Hop, House and Funk. It was common in the mid- to late-1990s popular music charts, as summery and accessible. Tempo varies but it mixes well with House and speeded-up Hip Hop, with lively drums and strange samples.

Classic tracks
Ceasefire vs Deadly Avenger –
'Evil Knievel'
Chemical Brothers – 'Block Rockin' Beats'
Fatboy Slim – 'Everybody Needs a 303'
Freestylers – 'Ruffneck'

CHART

Whatever style is, or has just been, in the general pop music charts. It usually includes a sprinkling of classic rock, novelty songs by soap stars or children's TV puppets, boy bands, girl bands, girl-and-boy bands, boys or girls who have left bands to go solo and, increasingly, boys who have left boy bands because they would prefer to be girls, and vice versa. Chart is invaluable at mixed-age and non-club events.

Classic tracks
Consult the latest pop music
charts and the dance compilation
recordings at your high-street store.

CHEESE

Easy to recognize, but difficult to describe, Cheese is not a million miles from 'corn' – easy-going, undemanding, familiar with mass-market appeal based on a memorable chorus. Attractive to playgroups and grannies alike, it usually has a simple dance routine as seen on the promotional video. A good Cheese track creates groans at first, but soon folk of all ages are mouthing the words and doing the dance.

Classic tracks
Abba – 'Dancing Queen'
Bay City Rollers – 'Shang-a-Lang'
Damien – 'Time Warp'
Disco Tex and the Sex-O-Lettes – 'Get Dancing'
Jeff Beck – 'Hi Ho Silver Lining'
Los Del Mar – 'Macarena'
Nolans – I'm in the Mood for Dancing'
Norman Greenbaum – 'Spirit in the Sky'
Whigfield – 'Saturday Night'
(Never, ever, EVER 'The Birdie Song')

DISCO

Classic Disco dates from the 1970s as seen on the movie *Saturday Night Fever* – glittery costumes, big hair, brass sections and 'syn drums' (synthesizer drums with a  whooshing or falling sound). Classic Disco is generally undemanding and tolerated by most generations. Seventies events get away with playing nothing else, although they tend to blur true Disco with Abba etc.

Classic tracks
Abba (by default) – 'Waterloo'
Bee Gees – 'Stayin' Alive', 'Tragedy'
Chic – 'C'est Chic (Le Freak)'
Jacksons – 'Blame It on the Boogie'
O'Jays – 'Love Train'
Tramps – 'Disco Inferno'

DRUM 'n' BASS

A strange convergence of styles in the early 1990s, including double-speed Hip Hop, led to this style of mainly drums and bass (guitar). Due to its sparse nature and frantic high speed, Drum 'n' bass has remained a relatively inaccessible 'underground' sound. Its energy needs ridiculous volume, and its dark, intimidating face grew out of early Jungle and Hardcore into rapid-paced, scary mayhem.

Classic tracks
Bad Company – 'The Nine'
Mickey Finn & Aphrodite – 'Bad Ass'
Moving Fusion – 'The Beginning'
Q-Project – 'Champion Sound'
Goldie – 'Inner City Life'
Roni Size – 'Brown Paper Bag'

EIGHTIES

Many music styles began in the 1980s, which also saw rising superstars such as Michael Jackson and Madonna. More narrowly, Eighties refers to the highly groomed and styled synthesizer-based bands of the New Romantic era, especially Duran Duran, Spandau Ballet, Human League and Visage. Eighties is often remembered fondly, but as a form of nostalgia, rather than for any real dance power.

GABBA

This outrageous, ultra-fast (sometimes > 300 beats-per-minute) style of extreme Hardcore is mainly from continental Europe. It can, and usually does, sound utterly ridiculous to the uninterested ear, consisting basically of a manic booming drum beat. See also Hardcore and Happy Hardcore.

GARAGE

Allegedly named after New York club the Paradise Garage, rather than being a poor relation of House music, Garage is a relatively lively, slinky, sexy and easy-dancing alternative to House and Trance. Ayia Napa makes Cyprus the Garage holiday island (Ibiza is more Trance and House) and a favoured DJ-ing summer destination. It's a popular remix style, especially for R&B tunes.

> **Classic tracks**
> Artful Dodger – 'Rewind'
> DJ Zinc – '138 Trek'
> MJ Cole – 'Sincere'
> Shanks and Bigfoot – 'Sweet Like Chocolate'

HARD HOUSE

A relatively new style, HH is a cross-breed of House, Techno and Trance. It is popular with clubbers as energetic and fast (about  140 beats-per-minute). As the early 2000s arrived, so did HH, although it can be mistaken for European Techno of the early and mid-1990s. It's a growing genre that attracts many new DJs.

> **Classic tracks**
> Bulletproof – 'Say Yeah'
> Public Domain – 'Operation Blade'
> Tony de Vit – 'The Dawn'

HARDCORE/HAPPY HARDCORE

Also known as 4-beat, Hardcore is noisy and fast – up to 180 beats-per-minute – and often too rapid for comfortable dancing. It will probably remain hard to accept for the general public. But its variant, Happy Hardcore, is a fraction slower and often incorporates piano riffs, comic vocals and remixes of old TV themes such as *Sesame Street*, hence the 'Happy'. See also Old Skool.

Classic tracks
Luna C – 'Piano Progression'
Red Alert & Mike Slammer – 'Let's Do It'
Seduction – 'Everybody'
Slipmatt – 'Breakin' Free'

HIP HOP

The term was invented by Afrika Bambaata, early leader of the 'Zulu Nation' black society in New York, USA. Originally a culture of the South Bronx around the mid-1970s, where mainly black youth expressed themselves in graffiti art, break-dancing and rapping. Godfathers of Hip Hop such as Grandmaster Flash, Cash Money and Kool Herc manipulated soul and funk records using two turntables and a mixer, playing drum breaks continuously so that people could rap or scratch over the top. Much of modern urban youth culture owes a debt to Hip Hop and Rap, and these styles have sold billions.

Classic tracks
Eminem – 'Slim Shady'
Coolio – 'Gangsta's Paradise'
Fugees – 'Ready or Not'
Kurtis Blow – 'The Breaks'
Sugar Hill Gang – 'Rapper's Delight'

HOUSE

House is what many people imagine as 'club dance music'. Acid House evolved as new electronic beats appeared, especially in Chicago – the term 'Chicago House' is still heard today. Now ubiquitous in club and chart, it's about 120-ish beats-per-minute, smoothly energetic, sometimes almost exciting, with a standard 4/4 beat, usually electronic, decorated by raps, samples and almost anything else.

Classic tracks
Bass-O-Matic – 'Fascinating Rhythm'
CJ Bolland – 'Sugar is Sweeter'
K-Klass – 'Let Me Show You'
Mr Fingers – 'Can You Feel It?'
The Bucketheads – 'The Bomb'

JUNGLE

A close relative or even twin of Drum 'n' bass, pure 'original' Jungle experienced its glory years in the early to mid-1990s, as the rave scene and Old Skool waned. It drew on Jamaican-style rapping and MC-ing, with crazy tribal drum patterns and speaker-shattering bass. Today it continues to evolve mainly alongside Drum 'n' bass.

Classic tracks
Congo Natty – 'Code Red'
DJ Krome and Mr Time – 'The Licence'
DJ Zinc – 'Fugees or Not?'
Shy FX & UK Apache – 'Original Nuttah'

OLD SKOOL

Old Skool was a major style in
the secretly organized
'raves' of the early 1990s. It
has plenty of drums and
bass guitar, often with
cartoony vocals and rapid,
cheesy piano riffs. It is still popular at large
outdoor parties and has encouraged Jungle,
UK Garage, Drum 'n' Bass and Hardcore. Some
of the world's biggest dance acts, such as The
Prodigy, owe much to its success.

Classic tracks
Blame – 'Music Takes You'
Omni Trio – 'Renegade Snares'
SL2 – 'On a Ragga Tip'
The Prodigy – 'Everybody in the Place'
Urban Shakedown – 'Some Justice'

RAP

Rappers talk the message in rhythm and
rhyme. The backbeat is drum-based, other
musical instruments are sparse. It sounds
simple – until you hear an unskilled rapper
and cringe. The style solidified in the early

1980s, but has diversified hugely since. It can merge with Hip Hop or spread into Gangsta (aimed squarely at authority), true hardcore rap, or the mass-appeal pop version with pretty boys in shiny, baggy pants.

> **Classic tracks**
> Public Enemy – 'Rebel without a Pause'
> Grandmaster Flash and the Furious Five – 'The Message'
> Missy Elliott – 'Supa Dupa Fly'
> Mobb Deep – 'The Infamous'

RAVE

Often used for the name of an event, as in 'a rave', rather like 'a thrash' or 'a hoe-down'. See Old Skool.

R&B (older)

The older, traditional style of Rhythm 'n' Blues lies somewhere between 12-Bar Blues and Rock 'n' Roll, with a solid boogie beat, wailing slide guitar, lashings of harmonica, and a singer who wakes up this morning and has himself a beer.

R&B (newer)

Today's R&B music and its female superstars are swinging, slowish, sexy, slinky, good-looking, glossy, chart-friendly – and massively popular. R&B sometimes fuses with Rap and Hip Hop, and like most styles, it has a big commercial side and a lesser underground face. High-budget videos and lavish production are regularly tied into major movie releases (*Charlie's Angels*, *Moulin Rouge*).

Classic tracks
Destiny's Child – 'Survivor'
All Saints – 'Lady Marmalade'
Missy Elliott – 'Get Your Freak On'
Usher – 'Pop Ya Collar'

ROCK

Rock still has a large following at pubs, clubs and stadium gigs. It can be heavy, middle-of-the-road (MOR), glam, punk, country, adult-orientated (AOR) or 'n' Roll. But it's still mainly guitars, often keyboards, with bass guitar and drums laying down a 4/4 beat – and all played by humans. At mixed-age events, Rock can please 'non-clubber' guests who despair of the incessant bang-bang of dance music.

Classic tracks

Bon Jovi – 'Livin' on a Prayer'
Bryan Adams – 'The Only Thing that Looks Good on Me'
Foreigner – 'More than a Feeling'
Golden Earring – 'Radar Love'
Led Zeppelin – 'Whole Lotta Love'
Motorhead – 'Ace of Spades'
Mud – 'Tiger Feet'
Queen – 'Bohemian Rhapsody'
Rolling Stones – 'Brown Sugar'
Sweet – 'Blockbuster'
T Rex – '20th Century Boy'

SEVENTIES

See Disco. Apart from classic US Disco, other 1970s styles still popular here and there are Glam and Punk. See Rock.

SIXTIES

The original 'pop' decade, the Sixties may embarrass today's clubbers – partly because their parents dance to it. But many styles and some of the world's most enduring tunes originated then – Beach Boys, Rolling Stones, soul, funk, Tamla Motown and the honkin' horns of Atlantic and Stax. Oddly, records from the world's biggest-ever pop band, the Beatles, are strangely un-danceable (with the notable exception of 'Get Back').

Classic tracks
Chris Montez – 'Let's Dance' (pop)
James Brown – 'Papa's Got a Brand New Bag' (soul)
Len Barry – '1-2-3' (pop)
Little Eva – 'The Locomotion' (wall-of-sound)
Rolling Stones – 'Satisfaction' (rock-blues)
Sly and the Family Stone – 'Dance to the Music' (funk)
Supremes – 'Baby Love' (Motown)

TECHNO

Techno is close to House, usually a trifle faster at around 140 beats-per-minute, and it has a more distorted, purely electronic style with fewer vocals. Its origins can be traced back to 808 State and New Order in the late 1980s, and Kraftwerk before that. It blends influences from Eurodance and the USA, especially the famous Detroit Techno sound.

Classic tracks
2 Unlimited – 'No Limits'
808 State – 'Cubik'
Lochi (Liberator DJs) – 'London Acid City'
New Order – 'Blue Monday'
Underworld – 'Born Slippy'

TRANCE

Trance has matured from its new-age-traveller links into one of the world's most popular types of dance music, thanks in no small part to the small Mediterranean island of Ibiza. It usually consists of spacey synthesizer melodies and warping, beepy noises, laid over a fairly quick Techno/House beat. It's a useful starter style for new DJs, being fairly easy to mix, with sunny sounds popular at parties.

> **Classic tracks**
> Binary Finary – '1998'
> Chicane – 'Offshore'
> Energy 52 – 'Cafe Del Mar'
> Faithless – 'Insomnia'
> Paul Van Dyk – 'For An Angel'
> System F – 'Out Of The Blue'

TRIP HOP

Primarily music for taking a break, Trip Hop's relaxing, quieting effect is used in club 'chill-rooms' where dancers cool down from the more aggressive styles played on the main dance floor. Many mainstream artists have Trip Hop influences or the occasional chill-out track on their albums, from British Indie band Portishead to Iceland's most famous export, Bjork.

> **Classic tracks**
> Coldcut – 'Beats and Pieces'
> DJ Food – 'Jazz Brakes'
> DJ Shadow – 'Endtroducing'
> Massive Attack – 'Teardrop'
> Tricky – 'Maxinquaye'

Glossary

WHAT THE $*@%! DOES THAT MEAN?

The world of DJ-ing is full of jargon and technical terms. Often, these aren't of much practical use. But they are essential for that most vital DJ trait – bluffing.

Feel free to make up new words, or adapt ordinary words to the music scene, and immediately gain the upper hand in any conversation. Then you can gaze with sympathy at people who don't understand what you are talking about. Even as they try to fathom out the meaning of your new, groovy-sound jargon word, you as the cunning DJ have already moved on, to make up another one.

Try combining parts of words already fashionable in other areas, like the Internet, Formula 1 motor racing, children's cartoons or exotic soups. Here are a few examples: Alstastant, Burdilt, Jispo, Malkagrid,

Puquillard, Tramble, Webreevous.

ACETATE Test pressing of a new track or recording that is physically weak and only lasts for a few plays.

BEAT-MIXING (often shortened to 'mixing') – Joining songs or musical pieces together with a continuous beat speed, with no change in the speed or rate of rhythm. See Tempo.

BPM Beats-per-minute, basically the speed of the music. See Tempo. Classic club Disco is around 120 to130 BPM (about two thumps or bangs per second).

BREAK Originally part of a record which is broken down, separated out or taken apart into the various instruments or sections, usually to leave only some thumping drums, throbbing bass or another underlying element of the rhythm.

CANS Headphones.

COFFIN A strong case that holds the basic DJ equipment of twos record decks and a mixer.

CROSSFADER Part of the mixer that controls which deck or track is being listened to. It is usually a sliding knob or button that moves sideways, from the position where only one deck can be heard, to the position where only the other deck can be heard. In between the two positions, the sound from one deck gradually lessens or fades down, while the other rises or fades up.

CUEING Lining up to enter somewhere. No, that's queuing. Cueing is getting a piece of music ready to play, from the beginning or from a certain place within it. Usually done by listening 'privately' under headphones.

DECKS Turntables or record players, usually for vinyl discs. Also known as ones and twos, or wheels of steel. Usually deck A is on the left, B is on the right. The term is also used for CD or DVD players, even audio tape or cassette players.

DIGITAL Really good. A form of audio recording in which sounds are stored as numbers, producing a purer sound

DISC Anything circular and flat. See Record. Could also be compact disc (CD), MiniDisc (MD) or even digital video disc (DVD). See Choose your format, page 45.

DJ Disc jockey. See Chapter 1.

DUB-PLATE Test version of a new recording, often played by DJs to see if the crowd responds favourably.

EQ Equalization. A row of sliders, knobs or buttons that alters the loudness of certain frequencies, or pitches, of the sound. EQ is really just a jumped-up version of the 'tone control' on an older record-player, with knobs labelled 'Bass' and 'Treble'. Since the row of 10 or more sliders on the EQ panel can be arranged to make a pretty wavy pattern, it's often called graphic EQ.

FADER Slider or knob on the mixer that controls the loudness or level of the music which is fed to the amplifiers and speakers. It can be an upfader, crossfader, etc. (In essence, a volume control.)

FLIPSIDE The side of a disc with the lesser-known song or track. Also called the B-side. On a CD (which has only one side), the tune which is less well-known than the others.

GIG Catch-all term for an event, venue or performance. For example: 'Did you catch my gig last night'? Pronounced with two hard g's, as in 'gargle'. 'Jig' or 'gij' or 'jij' will bring instant ridicule.

MC Master of Ceremonies. The person who announces what's happening when, or who urges listeners to do something, such as put their hands together, or give it up large for the next act. The MC can also be the DJ.

MIXER Mixing desk that controls the sound source being used, whether it is being fed through to the amplifiers and speakers and how loud it is. It's usually covered with knobs, switches, dials, buttons, sliders, faders, blood, sweat and tears.

PLATTER The circular, usually metal part of the deck (turntable) that supports the vinyl disc or record and spins around. See also Slipmat.

PRESSING Making a vinyl copy of a recording. The vinyl disc is 'pressed' using a metal version, the master disc.

PROMO Promotional version of a new recording. This is usually sent to DJs and other influential outlets such as producers, publicists and shops, often free as a form of advertising.

RAP To talk rather than sing, usually in rhyme and in rhythm.

RECORD See Disc, and Choose your format, page 45.

SAMPLING Stealing. Not really, it's taking an extract or piece from someone else's recording (with permission of course), and perhaps altering it electronically, then mixing or manipulating it into a new track.

SCRATCHING, SCRATCH-MIXING Moving the vinyl discs by hand while they are playing, to manipulate the beats, the sounds and the rhythm, and at the same time moving controls on the mixer to fade the sound up or down, or from one turntable deck to the other. See the feature on page 51.

SET The series of recordings or tunes played during a session. The DJ can work it out in advance, or make it up on the night, or do a combination of these.

SLIPMAT The piece of material that sits between the vinyl-disc recording and the platter of the turntable beneath. It's usually made from a type of felt and works as a mat under the disc, allowing a degree of slip. It allows you to move the disc by hand independently of the steadily rotating platter beneath, but when you release the disc, it 'grips' again and rotates steadily.

STYLUS Pointed 'needle' that follows the spiral groove or track in the vinyl-disc recording's surface, and vibrates to produce sounds. It must be replaced regularly or it will wear itself and the groove.

TEMPO The speed or rate of the rhythm. It can be assessed vaguely as fast, slow, etc., or put into a musical context as a 'slow ballad' or a 'fast jive', or measured precisely in BPM (see above).

VINYL Type of plastic used to make vinyl-disc recordings. The term is used as shorthand for 'vinyl-disc recording', that is, the disc itself, or for the format of the sound system: 'Are you CD or vinyl?'